Simple Guide to Angular JR

I0467225

Practical Guide

V. Telman

Guide to Angular

1.Introduction to Dart

Angular is a popular open-source frontend web development framework maintained by Google. It is used for building dynamic, single-page web applications. Angular utilizes TypeScript, a superset of JavaScript, to build applications with large codebases. It provides a set of tools and libraries that help developers create responsive and interactive web applications.

Angular was first released by Google in 2010 and has since undergone several major updates. The latest version, Angular 12, was released in May 2021. The framework has a large and active community of developers who contribute to its ongoing development and improvement.

Some key features of Angular include its use of two-way data binding, dependency injection, and modular code organization. Two-way data binding allows changes to be automatically reflected in both the model and the view, making it easier to keep data in sync. Dependency injection helps manage the dependencies between different components of an application, making it easier to test and refactor code. Angular also promotes the use of reusable components and services, allowing developers to create modular, maintainable code.

Angular is designed to work well with other frontend libraries and frameworks, such as Bootstrap and Angular Material. It also includes built-in support for routing, form handling, and HTTP requests, making it easier to build feature-rich web applications. Additionally, Angular provides tools for unit testing and end-to-end testing, helping developers ensure the quality and reliability of their code.

Overall, Angular is a powerful framework for building modern web applications. With its rich set of features and strong community support, it has become a popular choice for developers looking to create robust, responsive web applications.

2.Setting up Angular

Setting up Angular involves a few key steps, starting with installing Node.js and npm. Node.js is a JavaScript runtime that allows you to run JavaScript on the server side, and npm is a package manager for Node.js that helps you install libraries and tools.

To install Node.js, you can download the installer from the official Node.js website and follow the installation instructions. Once Node.js is installed, npm will also be installed automatically.

Next, you'll need to install Angular CLI (Command Line Interface), which is a powerful tool for creating, managing, building, and testing Angular applications. To install Angular CLI, you can run the following command in your terminal:

```
```

npm install -g @angular/cli
```
```

This will install Angular CLI globally on your system, allowing you to access it from any directory. Once Angular CLI is installed, you can use it to create a new Angular project.

To create a new Angular project, you can run the following command in your terminal:

```
ng new my-angular-project
```

This will create a new Angular project with the name "my-angular-project" in the current directory. Angular CLI will set up the project structure, install all the necessary dependencies, and generate the initial files for your project.

After creating the project, you can navigate into the project directory and start the Angular development server by running the following command:

```
cd my-angular-project
ng serve
```

```
```

This will start the development server and compile your Angular project, allowing you to view it in your web browser at http://localhost:4200.

With Node.js, npm, Angular CLI, and a new Angular project set up, you are now ready to start developing your Angular application. You can begin by editing the generated files in the project directory and using Angular CLI commands to generate components, services, and more as needed.

3. Angular Components

In Angular, components are the building blocks of an application. Components encapsulate the HTML, CSS, and business logic of a particular part of the user interface. They promote reusability and maintainability by breaking down the application into smaller, modular pieces.

Creating components:

To create a component in Angular, you use the `@Component` decorator along with a TypeScript class. The `@Component` decorator allows you to specify the metadata for the component, such as the selector, template, and styles.

Here's an example of creating a simple component in Angular:

```typescript
import { Component } from '@angular/core';

@Component({
```

```
    selector: 'app-example',
    template: '<h1>Hello, Angular!</h1>',
    styles: ['h1 { color: blue; }']
})
export class ExampleComponent {}
```

In this example, we have created a component with the selector `app-example`, a template with a simple heading, and a style to change the color of the heading to blue.

Passing data to components:

One of the key features of components in Angular is the ability to pass data into a component from its parent component. This is typically done using input properties.

Here's an example of passing data to a component in Angular:

```typescript
import { Component, Input } from '@angular/core';

@Component({
```

```
  selector: 'app-greeting',
  template: '<h1>Hello, {{name}}!</h1>'
})
export class GreetingComponent {
  @Input() name: string;
}
```

In this example, we have created a `GreetingComponent` with an input property `name`. We can then pass the name value from the parent component like this:

```html
<app-greeting [name]="'Alice'"></app-greeting>
```

Nesting components:

Another powerful feature of Angular components is the ability to nest components within each other to create complex user interfaces. This is achieved by adding a component's selector within the template of another component.

Here's an example of nesting components in Angular:

```typescript
import { Component } from '@angular/core';

@Component({
  selector: 'app-parent',
  template: '<app-child></app-child>'
})
export class ParentComponent {}

@Component({
  selector: 'app-child',
  template: '<h1>Child Component</h1>'
})
export class ChildComponent {}
```

In this example, we have a `ParentComponent` that nests a `ChildComponent` within its template. When the `ParentComponent` is rendered, the `ChildComponent` will also be displayed within it.

Component lifecycle hooks:

Angular provides several lifecycle hooks that allow you to tap into key moments in a component's lifecycle. These hooks provide opportunities to perform actions at various stages, such as when the component is created, rendered, or destroyed.

Here are some of the most common lifecycle hooks in Angular:

1. `ngOnChanges`: Called when any data-bound input properties of the component change.
2. `ngOnInit`: Called once when the component is initialized.
3. `ngOnDestroy`: Called when the component is being destroyed.
4. `ngAfterViewInit`: Called after the component's view has been initialized.
5. `ngAfterContentInit`: Called after external content has been projected into the component.

Here's an example of using the `ngOnInit` lifecycle hook in Angular:

```typescript
```

```
import { Component, OnInit } from
'@angular/core';

@Component({
  selector: 'app-lifecycle',
  template: '<h1>Component Lifecylce
Hooks</h1>'
})
export class LifecycleComponent implements
OnInit {
  ngOnInit() {
    console.log('Component initialized');
  }
}
```

In this example, the `OnInit` interface is implemented to use the `ngOnInit` lifecycle hook, which will log a message to the console when the component is initialized.

By mastering Angular components and their key concepts like creating components, passing data, nesting components, and using lifecycle hooks, you can build powerful and dynamic applications with Angular.

4.Angular Directives are markers on a DOM

Angular Directives are markers on a DOM element that tell Angular to do something with that element. Angular comes with a variety of built-in directives that can be used to manipulate the DOM and create dynamic web applications. Additionally, developers can also create custom directives to further extend the functionality of their Angular applications.

Using built-in directives is a common practice in Angular development. Some of the most commonly used built-in directives include ngModel, ngFor, and ngIf.

The ngModel directive is used for two-way data binding between form controls and Angular components. It allows you to bind the value of an input field to a variable in your component, so that any changes to the input field are automatically reflected in the component and vice versa. For example, you can use ngModel in a form to bind the value of an input field to a variable named 'username' in your component:

```
<input type="text" [(ngModel)]="username">
```

The ngFor directive is used to iterate over a collection of data and render a template for each item in the collection. For example, you can use ngFor to display a list of items stored in an array called 'items' in your component:

```
<li *ngFor="let item of items">{{ item }}</li>
```

The ngIf directive is used to conditionally render elements in the DOM based on a specific condition. For example, you can use ngIf to display a message only if a variable named 'isLoggedIn' is set to true in your component:

```
<div *ngIf="isLoggedIn">Welcome, User!</div>
```

```
```

In addition to using built-in directives, developers can also create custom directives to encapsulate and reuse logic throughout their Angular applications. Custom directives can be used to abstract complex behavior into reusable components, improve code readability, and promote code reusability.

Creating a custom directive in Angular involves defining a class that implements the Directive interface and decorating it with the @Directive decorator. Within the directive class, you can define the logic for manipulating the DOM elements that the directive is applied to. For example, let's create a custom directive called 'appHighlight' that changes the background color of an element when it is hovered over:

```
import { Directive, ElementRef, HostListener } from '@angular/core';

@Directive({
  selector: '[appHighlight]'
```

```
})
export class HighlightDirective {
  constructor(private el: ElementRef) {}

  @HostListener('mouseenter')
  onMouseEnter() {
    this.highlight('yellow');
  }

  @HostListener('mouseleave')
  onMouseLeave() {
    this.highlight(null);
  }

  private highlight(color: string) {

this.el.nativeElement.style.backgroundColor =
color;
  }
}
```

To use the custom 'appHighlight' directive in a component template, you can simply add it as an attribute to the element you want to apply the directive to:

```
<p appHighlight>Hover over me to see the
background color change!</p>
```

In this example, the custom directive 'appHighlight' changes the background color of a paragraph element to yellow when the mouse hovers over it, and resets it to the default color when the mouse leaves.

Overall, Angular Directives are powerful tools that allow developers to manipulate the DOM, create dynamic web applications, and promote code reusability. By leveraging both built-in directives and custom directives, developers can efficiently build complex and interactive Angular applications.

5.Angular services

Angular services are a fundamental aspect of Angular applications. They are used to encapsulate reusable functionality that can be shared between different components in an Angular application. Services are commonly used to interact with backend APIs, perform data manipulation, or handle any other business logic that needs to be shared across multiple components.

Creating services in Angular is a straightforward process. To create a new service, you can use the Angular CLI command `ng generate service <service-name>`. This command will create a new service file in the `src/app` directory of your Angular project. Inside the service file, you can define the functionality that the service will provide.

For example, let's say we want to create a simple service that provides a method to calculate the square of a number. We can create a new `CalculatorService` by running the following command:

```
ng generate service calculator
```

This will generate a new service file named `calculator.service.ts` in the `src/app` directory. Inside this file, we can define a method called `calculateSquare` that takes a number as an argument and returns the square of that number.

```typescript
import { Injectable } from '@angular/core';

@Injectable({
  providedIn: 'root'
})
export class CalculatorService {

  calculateSquare(num: number): number {
    return num * num;
  }
}
```

Once the service has been created, we need to register it with the Angular dependency injection system so that it can be injected into components that need to use it. This is done by providing the service in the `@Injectable` decorator in the service file with the `providedIn: 'root'` option.

Dependency injection in Angular allows us to inject a service into a component or another service without having to manually create an instance of that service. This makes our code more modular and easier to test. To inject a service into a component, we simply need to declare a constructor parameter of the service type in the component class.

For example, let's create a new component called `CalculatorComponent` that uses the `CalculatorService` we created earlier to calculate the square of a number. We can inject the `CalculatorService` into the `CalculatorComponent` as follows:

```typescript
import { Component } from '@angular/core';
import { CalculatorService } from
```

```
'./calculator.service';

@Component({
  selector: 'app-calculator',
  template: `
    <h2>Square of 5 is {{ square }}</h2>
  `
})
export class CalculatorComponent {

  square: number;

  constructor(private calculatorService:
CalculatorService) {
    this.square =
this.calculatorService.calculateSquare(5);
  }
}
```

In this example, we have injected the
`CalculatorService` into the
`CalculatorComponent` by declaring a
constructor parameter of type
`CalculatorService`. We then use the
`calculatorService` to calculate the square of
the number 5 and assign it to the `square`

property, which is displayed in the component template.

Consuming services in Angular components is a powerful way to share functionality across different parts of an Angular application. By creating services, registering them with the Angular dependency injection system, and injecting them into components, we can easily reuse code and keep our application organized and maintainable.

6. Routing in Angular

Routing in Angular is an essential part of building a single-page application (SPA) that provides a seamless user experience by allowing users to navigate between different views within the application. In Angular, routing is handled by the RouterModule, which provides a way to map URL paths to components.

Setting up routes in Angular involves configuring the routes in the AppModule or a separate module. This can be done using the RouterModule.forRoot() method to define the routes for the root module or RouterModule.forChild() for feature modules. Each route is defined using a JavaScript object that specifies the path to the route and the component that should be displayed when the route is accessed.

For example, to set up routes for a simple Angular application with two components, HomeComponent and AboutComponent, the

AppRoutingModule could look like this:

```typescript
import { NgModule } from '@angular/core';
import { Routes, RouterModule } from
'@angular/router';
import { HomeComponent } from
'./home.component';
import { AboutComponent } from
'./about.component';

const routes: Routes = [
  { path: 'home', component: HomeComponent
},
  { path: 'about', component: AboutComponent
},
];

@NgModule({
  imports: [RouterModule.forRoot(routes)],
  exports: [RouterModule]
})
export class AppRoutingModule { }
```

In this example, when the user navigates to
'/home', the HomeComponent will be

displayed, and when the user navigates to '/about', the AboutComponent will be displayed.

Route parameters allow for dynamic routing in Angular, where the path includes parameters that can be extracted and used to display specific content. Route parameters are denoted by a colon (:) followed by the parameter name in the route path definition.

For example, to set up a route with a parameter that represents a user's ID, the route definition would look like this:

```typescript
const routes: Routes = [
  { path: 'user/:id', component: UserComponent },
];
```

In this example, when the user navigates to '/user/123', the UserComponent will be displayed, and the value '123' will be available as the id parameter in the component.

Nested routes in Angular allow for creating hierarchical navigation structures where components are displayed inside other components. This is useful for building complex layouts with nested views and navigating between different levels of the application.

To set up nested routes in Angular, the child routes are defined within the route configuration of the parent component. Each child route is specified using the children property, which contains an array of route definitions.

For example, to set up nested routes for a DashboardComponent with child routes for different sections, the route configuration would look like this:

```typescript
const routes: Routes = [
  { path: 'dashboard', component: DashboardComponent, children: [
    { path: 'overview', component: OverviewComponent },
    { path: 'analytics', component:
```

```
AnalyticsComponent },
    { path: 'settings', component:
SettingsComponent },
  ]},
];
```
```

In this example, when the user navigates to '/dashboard', the DashboardComponent will be displayed, and the child routes 'overview', 'analytics', and 'settings' will determine which component is displayed inside the DashboardComponent.

Overall, routing in Angular is a powerful feature that enables developers to create rich user experiences with seamless navigation between different views. By setting up routes, using route parameters, and implementing nested routes, Angular applications can provide a smooth and intuitive user interface that enhances the overall user experience.
```

7.Forms in Angular

Angular is a powerful front-end framework that allows developers to create dynamic and interactive web applications. One of the key features of Angular is its support for forms. There are two main ways to implement forms in Angular: template-driven forms and reactive forms.

Template-driven forms are a simpler and more intuitive way to create forms in Angular. These forms are defined directly in the HTML template using directives such as ngModel, ngForm, and ngSubmit. The form controls are bound directly to properties in the component class, enabling two-way data binding between the form controls and the component.

Here's an example of a simple template-driven form in Angular:

```html
<form #myForm="ngForm"
(ngSubmit)="submitForm(myForm)">
  <input type="text" name="name" ngModel
```

```
required>
  <input type="email" name="email" ngModel
required email>
  <button type="submit">Submit</button>
</form>
```

In this example, we have a form with two input fields for name and email. The ngModel directive is used to bind the input values to properties in the component class. The required and email validators are used to enforce validation rules on the form controls.

Reactive forms, on the other hand, are more complex but offer more flexibility and control over form validation and submission. Reactive forms are created programmatically in the component class using FormBuilder and FormGroup classes. Form controls are defined as FormControl instances and grouped together in a FormGroup or FormArray.

Here's an example of a simple reactive form in Angular:

```typescript
```

```typescript
import { Component, OnInit } from
'@angular/core';
import { FormBuilder, FormGroup, Validators
} from '@angular/forms';

@Component({
  selector: 'app-my-form',
  templateUrl: './my-form.component.html',
  styleUrls: ['./my-form.component.css']
})
export class MyFormComponent implements
OnInit {

  myForm: FormGroup;

  constructor(private fb: FormBuilder) {}

  ngOnInit(): void {
    this.myForm = this.fb.group({
      name: ['', Validators.required],
      email: ['', [Validators.required,
Validators.email]]
    });
  }

  submitForm(): void {
    if (this.myForm.valid) {
```

```
    console.log(this.myForm.value);
  }
 }


}
```
```

In this example, we define a reactive form with two form controls for name and email using the FormBuilder service. Validators are applied to enforce validation rules on the form controls. The form is then attached to the template usingformGroup directive.

Validations are an important part of forms in Angular to ensure that user input is correct and meets the specified criteria. There are several built-in validators in Angular that can be used to enforce validation rules on form controls. Some common validators include required, minLength, maxLength, pattern, and email.

Here's an example of how to apply validators to form controls in Angular:

```typescript

```typescript
import { Component } from '@angular/core';
import { FormControl, FormGroup,
Validators } from '@angular/forms';

@Component({
  selector: 'app-my-form',
  templateUrl: './my-form.component.html',
  styleUrls: ['./my-form.component.css']
})
export class MyFormComponent {

  myForm = new FormGroup({
    name: new FormControl('',
[Validators.required,
Validators.minLength(3)]),
    email: new FormControl('',
[Validators.required, Validators.email])
  });

  submitForm(): void {
    if (this.myForm.valid) {
      console.log(this.myForm.value);
    }
  }

}
```
```
```

In this example, we define a reactive form with two form controls for name and email. Validators.required and Validators.minLength are used to enforce validation rules on the name control, while Validators.required and Validators.email are used for the email control. The form is then submitted only if all validation rules are met.

Overall, forms in Angular provide a powerful and flexible way to handle user input and validation in web applications. Whether you choose template-driven forms or reactive forms, Angular provides the tools and functionality to create robust and interactive forms for your applications.

8. HTTP Client in Angular

Angular provides a built-in HTTP client module that allows us to easily make HTTP requests to backend services. In this guide, we will learn how to use the HttpClient module to send HTTP requests, handle responses, and handle errors in an Angular application.

Making HTTP requests:

To make HTTP requests in Angular, we need to import the HttpClient module from the @angular/common/http package. We can then inject the HttpClient service into our components or services to send HTTP requests.

Here is an example of how we can make a GET request to fetch data from a backend API:

```typescript
import { HttpClient } from '@angular/common/http';
```

```
@Injectable()
export class DataService {
  constructor(private http: HttpClient) {}

  getData() {
    return
this.http.get('https://api.example.com/data');
  }
}
```

In the above code snippet, we have created a DataService class that injects the HttpClient service and defines a method called `getData()` that sends a GET request to `https://api.example.com/data`.

Handling responses:

When the HTTP request is successful, the `get()` method returns an Observable of the HTTP response. We can then subscribe to this Observable to handle the response data.

Here is an example of how we can handle the response data in our component:

```typescript
export class AppComponent implements
OnInit {
  data: any;

  constructor(private dataService:
DataService) {}

  ngOnInit() {

this.dataService.getData().subscribe((response
) => {
    this.data = response;
  });
 }
}
```

In the above code snippet, we have subscribed
to the Observable returned by the `getData()`
method and assigned the response data to the
`data` property.

Error handling:

In addition to handling successful responses, it
is also important to handle errors that may

occur during the HTTP request. We can use the `catchError` operator from the RxJS library to handle errors in Angular.

Here is an example of how we can handle errors in our DataService class:

```typescript
import { catchError } from 'rxjs/operators';

@Injectable()
export class DataService {
  constructor(private http: HttpClient) {}

  getData() {
    return this.http.get('https://api.example.com/data').pipe(
      catchError((error) => {
        console.error('Error fetching data:', error);
        throw error;
      })
    );
  }
}
```

In the above code snippet, we have used the `catchError` operator to catch any errors that occur during the HTTP request. We have also logged the error using `console.error` and re-thrown the error for further handling.

The HttpClient module in Angular provides a convenient way to make HTTP requests, handle responses, and handle errors in our applications. By following the examples and best practices outlined in this guide, we can effectively work with HTTP requests in Angular applications.

9.Angular Modules:

Understanding and Creating Them

Angular is a powerful JavaScript framework designed for building web applications. One of its core concepts is the module system, which helps organize and encapsulate the application's functionality. This article will delve deep into understanding Angular modules and provide comprehensive guidance on creating and importing them.

Understanding Angular Modules

What Are Angular Modules?

In Angular, a module is a container for a cohesive block of code dedicated to an application domain, a workflow, or a closely related set of capabilities. Angular uses a modular architecture that enables separation of concerns and reusability of code. Modules group components, directives, pipes, and services that are related to a specific feature.

Core Concepts of Angular Modules

1. **NgModule**: This is the class decorator that defines an Angular module. Each module in Angular is defined with the `@NgModule` decorator, which takes a metadata object.

2. **Declarations**: This array within the `@NgModule` decorator contains the components, directives, and pipes that belong to this module.

3. **Imports**: This array lists other modules that are needed by components in this module. Any module you want to use in your declarations must be imported.

4. **Providers**: This array defines services that will be instantiated by the Angular injector for this module. It allows sharing services across components in the module.

5. **Bootstrap**: This array is used in the root module to define the main application view, called the root component. Angular uses this component to launch the application.

6. **Exports**: This array is for sharing components, directives, and pipes with the

components of other modules.

Example of an Angular Module

Here is a simple example to illustrate the structure of an Angular module:

```typescript
import { NgModule } from '@angular/core';
import { BrowserModule } from
'@angular/platform-browser';
import { AppComponent } from
'./app.component';
import { HelloWorldComponent } from
'./hello-world.component';

@NgModule({
  declarations: [
    AppComponent,
    HelloWorldComponent  // Declare
components here
  ],
  imports: [
    BrowserModule  // Import necessary
modules here
  ],
  providers: [],
```

```
  bootstrap: [AppComponent]  // Bootstrap the
root component
})
export class AppModule { }
```
```

### Advantages of Using Modules

- **Separation of Concerns**: Modules help in organizing code into cohesive blocks, making it easier to manage and understand.

- **Lazy Loading**: Modules can be lazy-loaded, meaning that they can be loaded on demand, which helps in reducing the initial load time of the application.

- **Reusability**: You can create reusable modules that can be imported into other modules, promoting code DRYness (Don't Repeat Yourself).

- **Scalability**: As applications grow, modules help in scaling the project structure and organization, facilitating better collaboration among developers.
```

Creating Angular Modules

Creating a module in Angular involves a few straightforward steps.

Step-by-Step Guide

1. **Generate a Module**: You can create a module using Angular CLI. Open your terminal and run:

    ```bash
    ng generate module my-new-module
    ```

    This command creates a new folder named `my-new-module` with a file called `my-new-module.module.ts`.

2. **Define the Module**: Open `my-new-module.module.ts` and define the module using the `@NgModule` decorator. Here's an example:

    ```typescript
    import { NgModule } from '@angular/core';
    import { CommonModule } from
    ```

```typescript
'@angular/common';
import { MyNewComponent } from './my-new-component/my-new.component';

@NgModule({
  declarations: [
    MyNewComponent // Declare your components here
  ],
  imports: [
    CommonModule // Import other common modules
  ],
  exports: [
    MyNewComponent // Export your components if needed
  ]
})
export class MyNewModule { }
```

3. **Create a Component in the Module**: You may want to create a component that belongs to your new module:

```bash
ng generate component my-new-
```

module/my-new-component
```
```

This command generates a new component within the `my-new-module` directory.

4. **Use the Module**: To use the newly created module, you need to import it into another module, typically a parent or root module. Open `app.module.ts` and modify it as follows:

```typescript
import { NgModule } from '@angular/core';
import { BrowserModule } from '@angular/platform-browser';
import { AppComponent } from './app.component';
import { MyNewModule } from './my-new-module/my-new-module.module'; // Import your newly created module

@NgModule({
  declarations: [
    AppComponent
  ],
  imports: [
```

```
      BrowserModule,
      MyNewModule  // Include the new
module here
    ],
    providers: [],
    bootstrap: [AppComponent]
  })
  export class AppModule { }
```

5. **Use the Component**: Now, you can use
the component from `MyNewModule` in your
`AppComponent` template. For example, in
`app.component.html`:

```html
<h1>Welcome to My Angular App</h1>
<app-my-new-component></app-my-new-
component>  <!-- Use the component -->
```

Best Practices for Creating Modules

- **Module Naming**: Use meaningful
names for modules that reflect their
functionality. This helps in understanding the
application structure.

- **Feature Modules vs. Core Modules**: Consider creating feature modules for specific functionalities (e.g., UserModule, AdminModule) and a Core Module for singleton services used across the application.

- **Avoid Circular Dependencies**: Be mindful of how you import modules to prevent circular dependencies, which can lead to runtime errors.

- **Utilize Lazy Loading**: For large applications, consider implementing lazy loading for feature modules to optimize performance.

Importing Modules

Importing modules is crucial for reusing the functionalities defined in different modules within your Angular application.

Importing a Module from Another Module

Suppose you've created a utility module `UtilityModule` that provides common utility services. Here's how you would import it into another module:

1. **Create Utility Module**:

```typescript
import { NgModule } from '@angular/core';

@NgModule({
  providers: [
    // This could include various utility services
  ]
})
export class UtilityModule { }
```

2. **Import Utility Module into Another Module**:

In `AppModule`:

```typescript
import { NgModule } from '@angular/core';
import { BrowserModule } from '@angular/platform-browser';
import { AppComponent } from
```

```
'./app.component';
    import { UtilityModule } from
'./utility.module';  // Import UtilityModule

    @NgModule({
      declarations: [
        AppComponent
      ],
      imports: [
        BrowserModule,
        UtilityModule  // Include UtilityModule
here
      ],
      providers: [],
      bootstrap: [AppComponent]
    })
    export class AppModule { }
    ```
```

### Key Takeaways for Importing Modules

- Ensure that the module you are trying to
import is properly exported in its module file.
- Use relative paths when importing modules,
and maintain an organized folder structure for
ease of access.
- Be cautious about what you export to restrict
```

component exposure unnecessarily.

In Angular, modules are instrumental in achieving a clean, maintainable, and scalable architecture. Understanding how to create and import modules will enhance your ability to build sophisticated applications using Angular. By adhering to best practices, developers can ensure that their applications remain organized, testable, and easier to extend or refactor in the future.

Mastering modules is a step toward becoming proficient in Angular, allowing you to leverage its full potential in developing dynamic web applications. Harness the power of modules, and watch your application grow in complexity and capability, all while ensuring that your code remains tidy and manageable.

10.Angular Best Practices

Angular is a powerful framework for building client-side applications using TypeScript. As applications grow in complexity, following best practices becomes crucial to maintain code quality, increase maintainability, and improve performance. In this article, we will explore best practices for naming conventions, code organization, and performance optimization.

Naming Conventions

Naming conventions play a pivotal role in maintaining clarity within your codebase. When developers follow coherent and consistent naming strategies, it enhances readability and reduces the cognitive load when returning to the code later.

1. Component Naming

- **Use PascalCase**: Component names should be in PascalCase. For example:
    ```typescript
    ```

```typescript
@Component({
  selector: 'app-user-profile',
  templateUrl: './user-
profile.component.html',
})
export class UserProfileComponent {}
```

- **Suffix with Component**: It's standard to append "Component" to the name of the component. This infers its purpose clearly:
```typescript
UserListComponent, HeaderComponent,
FooterComponent
```

2. Directive Naming

- **Use camelCase with the Prefix 'app'**: Use camelCase for directive names, and prefix them with 'app':
```typescript
@Directive({
  selector: '[appHighlight]'
})
export class HighlightDirective {}
```

3. Service Naming

- **Use the suffix 'Service'**: For services, always append "Service" to the name:
  ```typescript
  export class AuthService {}
  ```

4. Module Naming

- **Suffix with Module**: For Angular modules, use the suffix "Module":
  ```typescript
  @NgModule({
    declarations: [UserProfileComponent],
  })
  export class UserProfileModule {}
  ```

5. File Naming

- **Follow your TypeScript Naming**: The filename should follow the same conventions as the class name. Use kebab-case for filenames:
  ```plaintext
```

```
user-profile.component.ts
auth.service.ts
user-profile.module.ts
```

Code Organization

Good code organization enhances maintainability and scalability. Structuring your Angular application efficiently will simplify future modifications and onboarding of new team members.

1. Feature Modules

Organize your application into modules based on features. For instance, if your application has components for user management, authentication, and product catalog, separate them into distinct modules. Each module should encapsulate its own components, services, and associated files.

```
/src
 /app
  /user
```

```
      user.module.ts
      user.component.ts
      user.service.ts
      user-profile.component.ts
    /auth
      auth.module.ts
      auth.service.ts
      login.component.ts
    /products
      products.module.ts
      product-list.component.ts
      product.service.ts
```

2. Shared Modules

Create a shared module for reusable
components, directives, and pipes. This helps
to avoid code duplication and fosters
reusability.

```typescript
@NgModule({
  declarations: [
    HeaderComponent,
    FooterComponent,
    HighlightDirective
```

```
  ],
  imports: [],
  exports: [
    HeaderComponent,
    FooterComponent,
    HighlightDirective
  ]
})
export class SharedModule {}
```

3. Core Module

Implement a core module to provide singleton services and components that are required throughout the app. This module should be imported only once in the AppModule.

```typescript
@NgModule({
  providers: [AuthService, LoggingService],
  imports: [SharedModule],
})
export class CoreModule {}
```

4. Smart and Dumb Components

Distinguish between smart (container) components that handle business logic and dumb (presentational) components that display the UI. This separation makes components easier to test and manage.

```typescript
// Smart Component
@Component({ templateUrl: 'user-list.component.html' })
export class UserListComponent {
  // Logic to fetch users
}

// Dumb Component
@Component({
  selector: 'app-user-card',
  template: `<div>{{ user.name }}</div>`
})
export class UserCardComponent {
  @Input() user: User;
}
```

Performance Optimization

Performance optimization is essential to provide a smooth user experience. Below are strategies to enhance the performance of your Angular application.

1. Lazy Loading Modules

Lazy loading allows you to load parts of your application only when needed. This can drastically reduce the initial load time. Use the Angular Router to implement lazy loading:

```typescript
const routes: Routes = [
  { path: 'users', loadChildren: () => import('./user/user.module').then(m => m.UserModule) },
];
```

2. OnPush Change Detection Strategy

By default, Angular follows the default change detection strategy. By using `OnPush`, Angular will only check the component and its children when an input property changes or an event occurs:

```typescript
@Component({
  selector: 'app-user-profile',
  changeDetection:
ChangeDetectionStrategy.OnPush
})
export class UserProfileComponent {}
```

3. TrackBy in ngFor

When using `*ngFor`, leverage the `trackBy` function to identify unique items in a list. This minimizes the DOM manipulations:

```html
<div *ngFor="let user of users; trackBy:
trackByUserId">
  {{ user.name }}
</div>
```

```typescript
trackByUserId(index: number, user: User):
number {
  return user.id; // or unique identifier
```

```
}
```

4. Avoid Unnecessary Pipes and Observables

Using pipes and observables in templates can lead to performance hits if not managed correctly. Avoid unnecessary computations in the template and subscribe to services in the component:

```typescript
this.userService.getUsers()
  .subscribe(users => this.users = users);
```

5. Use Angular CLI for Optimizations

Always run production builds using Angular CLI. The command `ng build --prod` enables Ahead-of-Time compilation, tree shaking, and minification, optimizing your code for production environments.

Following best practices in Angular – from naming conventions and code organization to performance optimization – can greatly enhance the maintainability and performance of your applications. Keeping your code clean and organized allows both you and other developers to work more effectively. By applying these strategies consistently, you can ensure an efficient workflow and a robust Angular application.

11. Testing in Angular:

An In-Depth Guide

Testing is a critical part of software development that ensures the reliability and functionality of your applications. In Angular, a popular framework for building web applications, testing is well-supported through various tools and methodologies. This guide will cover three fundamental aspects of testing in Angular: unit testing, end-to-end (E2E) testing, and writing testable code with practical examples to illustrate each concept.

Table of Contents

1. Introduction to Testing in Angular
2. Unit Testing
   - 2.1 What is Unit Testing?
   - 2.2 Setting Up Unit Tests in Angular
   - 2.3 Writing Unit Tests
   - 2.4 Common Testing Utilities
3. End-to-End Testing
   - 3.1 What is E2E Testing?
   - 3.2 Setting Up E2E Tests in Angular
   - 3.3 Writing E2E Tests
   - 3.4 Common E2E Testing Tools

4. Writing Testable Code
   - 4.1 Principles of Writing Testable Code
   - 4.2 Dependency Injection
   - 4.3 Separation of Concerns
5. Conclusion

1. Introduction to Testing in Angular

Angular provides a robust testing framework out of the box, integrating tools like Jasmine for unit testing and Protractor for E2E testing. Testing helps catch bugs early in the development cycle, assists in maintenance, and ensures that your application remains reliable as new features are added. Incorporating testing practices into your workflow enhances the quality of your application and improves developer productivity.

2. Unit Testing

2.1 What is Unit Testing?

Unit testing focuses on testing the smallest pieces of code, typically functions or methods, to ensure they work as intended. Each unit test is independent, allowing developers to isolate functionality and verify correctness. Unit tests are usually executed quickly, making them ideal for testing individual parts of an application.

2.2 Setting Up Unit Tests in Angular

Angular projects are created with the Angular CLI, which includes configuration for testing. Here's how to set it up:

1. **Create a new Angular project:**
   ```bash
   ng new my-angular-app
   cd my-angular-app
   ```

2. **Run the unit tests:**
   ```bash
   ng test
   ```

By default, Angular uses Jasmine as the testing framework and Karma as the test runner.

2.3 Writing Unit Tests

Here's a basic example of how to write a unit test for a service. Let's consider a simple calculator service:

```typescript
// calculator.service.ts
import { Injectable } from '@angular/core';

@Injectable({
  providedIn: 'root'
})
export class CalculatorService {
  add(a: number, b: number): number {
    return a + b;
  }

  subtract(a: number, b: number): number {
    return a - b;
  }
}
```

To test this service, you can create a corresponding test file:

```typescript
// calculator.service.spec.ts
import { TestBed } from
'@angular/core/testing';
import { CalculatorService } from
'./calculator.service';

describe('CalculatorService', () => {
  let service: CalculatorService;

  beforeEach(() => {
    TestBed.configureTestingModule({});
    service =
TestBed.inject(CalculatorService);
  });

  it('should add two numbers', () => {
    expect(service.add(1, 2)).toEqual(3);
  });

  it('should subtract two numbers', () => {
    expect(service.subtract(5, 2)).toEqual(3);
  });
});
```

2.4 Common Testing Utilities

- **Jasmine:** A behavior-driven development framework for testing JavaScript code.
- **Karma:** A test runner that allows you to run your tests in various real browsers.
- **Angular Testing Module (TestBed):** A powerful tool for configuring the testing environment.

3. End-to-End Testing

3.1 What is E2E Testing?

End-to-end (E2E) testing evaluates the application as a whole, ensuring that all components work together as expected. It mimics real user scenarios by interacting with the UI and validating outputs against expected results. E2E tests often take longer to run compared to unit tests, as they cover full workflows.

3.2 Setting Up E2E Tests in Angular

Angular automatically sets up E2E testing using Protractor when you generate a new project. To start E2E testing:

1. **Create a new Angular project with E2E support:**
   ```bash
   ng new my-angular-app --routing --style=scss
   ```

2. **Run the E2E tests:**
   ```bash
   ng e2e
   ```

3.3 Writing E2E Tests

Let's create an E2E test that checks if a user can successfully navigate to a specific route and see the correct heading.

```typescript
// e2e/src/app.e2e-spec.ts
import { browser, by, element } from 'protractor';

describe('My Angular App', () => {
  it('should display the correct heading on the
```

```
home page', () => {
    browser.get('/');
    let heading =
element(by.css('h1')).getText();
    expect(heading).toEqual('Welcome to My
Angular App!');
  });
});
```

3.4 Common E2E Testing Tools

- **Protractor:** An end-to-end test framework for Angular applications.
- **WebDriverJS:** The Selenium WebDriver JavaScript bindings that Protractor is built upon.
- **Cypress:** An alternative to Protractor that allows testing of modern web applications invariably.

4. Writing Testable Code

4.1 Principles of Writing Testable Code

To facilitate effective testing, developers should embrace certain principles when writing code. Here are some key recommendations:

- **Single Responsibility Principle:** Each class or function should have a single responsibility.
- **Dependency Injection:** Use dependency injection to make classes easily replaceable with mocks or stubs during testing.
- **Avoid Side Effects:** Functions should avoid changing the state of the application outside their scope.

4.2 Dependency Injection

In Angular, classes are made testable through dependency injection, allowing for the substitution of actual dependencies with mocks during tests.

Example of Dependency Injection:

```typescript
// user.service.ts
import { Injectable } from '@angular/core';

@Injectable({
```

```typescript
  providedIn: 'root'
})
export class UserService {
  getUser() {
    return { name: 'John Doe', age: 30 };
  }
}

// user.service.spec.ts
import { TestBed } from
'@angular/core/testing';
import { UserService } from './user.service';

describe('UserService', () => {
  let service: UserService;

  beforeEach(() => {
    TestBed.configureTestingModule({});
    service = TestBed.inject(UserService);
  });

  it('should return a user', () => {
    expect(service.getUser()).toEqual({ name:
'John Doe', age: 30 });
  });
});
```

4.3 Separation of Concerns

To prepare your code for testing, apply the separation of concerns:

- **Keep your business logic separate:** Use services to handle business logic and keep components focused solely on UI interactions.
- **Modular Design:** Break your application into smaller, manageable modules. This organization makes testing easier and more efficient.

5. Conclusion

Testing is an essential practice in Angular development that enhances code quality, promotes maintainability, and increases confidence in application behavior. By employing unit tests to verify individual components, E2E tests to check overall application functionality, and adhering to principles of writing testable code, developers can not only safeguard their applications against bugs but can also lay a foundation for future growth.

Adopting testing as a standard practice will ultimately lead to a more robust, maintainable, and scalable Angular application. With a rich ecosystem of tools and frameworks, Angular developers can efficiently implement different types of testing and ensure their applications meet both functional and non-functional requirements. Whether you are a seasoned developer or just starting, embracing testing in Angular will pay off in the long run.

12.Deployment of Angular Applications

Deploying a web application can often be one of the most critical phases of a development lifecycle. The deployment of an Angular application requires careful consideration of various factors including the build process, hosting environment, and continuous integration and delivery practices. This article will provide a comprehensive overview of deploying an Angular application, including the build process, hosting options, and CI/CD pipelines.

1. Building an Angular Application

Before hosting the Angular app, we need to build it. The Angular CLI simplifies the build process by providing commands that bundle the application efficiently. Here's a detailed exploration of the building phase:

Step 1: Set up Angular CLI

Ensure you have the Angular CLI installed. You can install Angular CLI globally using npm (Node Package Manager) by executing:

```bash
npm install -g @angular/cli
```

Step 2: Create an Angular Application

If you haven't already created an Angular application, you can do so with the following command:

```bash
ng new my-angular-app
```

This command creates a new folder named `my-angular-app` with a boilerplate Angular application.

Step 3: Configure Environment Files

Angular applications often have different configurations for development and production environments. In the `src/environments` folder, you will find two files: `environment.ts` for development and `environment.prod.ts` for production. Make sure to set the production configurations correctly, such as API endpoints.

Example of an environment file:

```typescript
// src/environments/environment.ts
export const environment = {
  production: false,
  apiUrl: 'http://localhost:3000/api'
};

// src/environments/environment.prod.ts
export const environment = {
  production: true,
  apiUrl: 'https://api.my-angular-app.com'
};
```

Step 4: Build the Application

To create a production build of your Angular application, run the following command:

```bash
ng build --prod
```

```
```

This command compiles the application and outputs the files into the `dist/my-angular-app` directory. The `--prod` flag activates optimizations intended for production use, such as Ahead-of-Time (AOT) compilation, minification, and uglification of your JavaScript code.

Example of Build Output

After executing the build command, you will find files like `index.html`, `main.js`, and `styles.css` in the `dist/my-angular-app` folder. The structure may look like this:

```
dist/
└── my-angular-app/
    ├── index.html
    ├── main-es2015.js
    ├── polyfills-es2015.js
    ├── runtime-es2015.js
    └── styles.css
```

2. Hosting on a Server

Once you've built the application, the next step is to host it on a server. There are various hosting options available, including cloud platforms like AWS, Azure, and Firebase. In this section, we will discuss:

Option 1: Hosting on an Apache Server

1. **Install Apache**

You first need an Apache server running on your environment. If you're using Ubuntu, you can install it using:

```bash
sudo apt-get update
sudo apt-get install apache2
```

2. **Copy Files to the Apache Root Directory**

After building your Angular application, copy the files from the `dist/my-angular-app` folder to the Apache server's root directory (usually

`/var/www/html`).

```bash
sudo cp -r dist/my-angular-app/*
/var/www/html/
```

3. **Set Up `.htaccess` for Routing**

Since Angular uses client-side routing, you
will need to set up an `.htaccess` file to
redirect all requests to `index.html`. Create a
file named `.htaccess` in the root of your
hosted files (`/var/www/html/`):

```plaintext
<IfModule mod_rewrite.c>
  RewriteEngine On
  RewriteBase /
  RewriteRule ^index\.html$ - [L]
  RewriteCond %
{REQUEST_FILENAME} !-f
  RewriteCond %
{REQUEST_FILENAME} !-d
  RewriteRule . /index.html [L]
</IfModule>
```

4. **Restart Apache**

After making the changes, restart Apache to apply the new configurations.

```bash
sudo systemctl restart apache2
```

Option 2: Hosting on Firebase

Firebase provides a fast and easy way to host web applications.

1. **Install Firebase CLI**

You can install Firebase CLI using npm:

```bash
npm install -g firebase-tools
```

2. **Login to Firebase**

Authenticate yourself through the Firebase CLI:

```bash
firebase login
```

3. **Initialize Firebase in Your App Directory**

In your Angular app's root directory, run:

```bash
firebase init
```

Select "Hosting" and follow the prompts to set up your Firebase project.

4. **Deploy Your Application**

Once you've configured Firebase, deploy your application using:

```bash
firebase deploy
```

Your Angular app will be hosted on Firebase,

and you will receive a URL where you can view your application.

3. Using CI/CD Pipelines

Continuous Integration (CI) and Continuous Deployment (CD) are essential processes for automating the release of your application. Here's a breakdown of setting up CI/CD pipelines for your Angular app:

Option 1: Using GitHub Actions

1. **Create a Workflow**

In your Angular application's repository, create a new directory named `.github/workflows` and create a YAML file named `ci-cd.yml` in that directory.

```yaml
name: CI/CD Pipeline

on:
  push:
    branches:
      - main
```

```yaml
jobs:
  build:
    runs-on: ubuntu-latest

    steps:
      - name: Checkout code
        uses: actions/checkout@v2

      - name: Set up Node.js
        uses: actions/setup-node@v2
        with:
          node-version: '14'

      - name: Install dependencies
        run: npm install

      - name: Build application
        run: npm run build --prod

      - name: Deploy to Firebase
        uses: wzieba/Firebase-Deployment-Github-Action@v2.2.0
        with:
          firebase_service_account: ${{ secrets.FIREBASE_SERVICE_ACCOUNT }}
```

```
    project_id: your_firebase_project_id
    cwd: ./dist/my-angular-app
```

2. **Configure Secrets in GitHub**

In your repository settings, add a secret named
`FIREBASE_SERVICE_ACCOUNT` with
your Firebase service account JSON. This
allows you to securely access Firebase during
deployment.

Option 2: Using CircleCI

1. **Create a Configuration File**

In the root of your project, create a file called
`.circleci/config.yml`.

```yaml
version: 2.1
jobs:
  build:
    docker:
      - image: circleci/node:14
    steps:
      - checkout
```

```
      - run:
          name: Install dependencies
          command: npm install
      - run:
          name: Build Application
          command: npm run build --prod
      - deploy:
          name: Deploy to Firebase
          command: firebase deploy --token
$FIREBASE_TOKEN

workflows:
  version: 2
  build_and_deploy:
    jobs:
      - build
```

2. **Set Environment Variables**

In the CircleCI project settings, add the `FIREBASE_TOKEN` environment variable, which you can obtain by running `firebase login:ci`.

Conclusion

Deploying an Angular application involves multiple stages, from building the application to selecting an appropriate hosting environment and implementing CI/CD pipelines. By following this comprehensive guide, you now have a foundational understanding of how to deploy your Angular applications effectively. Whether you choose to host on Apache, Firebase, or another platform, and whether you implement CI/CD with GitHub Actions or CircleCI, the key is to ensure your application is robust, scalable, and easy to maintain.

13.Advanced Topics in Angular

Angular is a robust framework developed by Google that allows developers to build rich and scalable web applications. As developers grow more comfortable with Angular, they often start delving into advanced topics that can enhance the performance, maintainability, and user experience of their applications. This document will explore three advanced topics in Angular: State Management with NgRx, Internationalization (i18n), and Universal (Server-Side Rendering). Each of these topics plays a critical role in building modern web applications that can meet the diverse needs of users and developers alike.

State Management with NgRx

What is NgRx?

NgRx is a powerful state management library for Angular applications inspired by the Redux library used in React applications. It provides a way to manage application state in a predictable manner by using the principles of the Redux pattern. NgRx provides a global store where the application state can be kept, and it goes beyond simple state management by introducing concepts such as Actions, Reducers, Effects, and Selectors.

Key Concepts of NgRx

1. **Store**: The central repository that holds the state of the application. It is an immutable object that represents the application state. Changes to the state are made through actions which are dispatched to the store.

2. **Actions**: Actions are plain JavaScript objects that describe "what happened" in the application. Each action has a `type` property used to identify the action and optionally carries a `payload` of data.

```typescript
import { createAction, props } from '@ngrx/store';

export const loadItems = createAction('[Item List] Load Items');
export const loadItemsSuccess =
```

```typescript
createAction(
  '[Item List] Load Items Success',
  props<{ items: Item[] }>()
);
```

3. **Reducers**: Reducers are pure functions that take the current state and an action as arguments, and return a new state. They specify how the state changes in response to an action.

```typescript
import { createReducer, on } from '@ngrx/store';
import { loadItemsSuccess } from './item.actions';

export const initialState: ItemState = {
  items: [],
  loading: false
};

const itemReducer = createReducer(
  initialState,
  on(loadItemsSuccess, (state, { items }) =>
({
```

```typescript
    ...state,
    items: items
  }))
);

export function reducer(state: ItemState |
undefined, action: Action) {
  return itemReducer(state, action);
}
```

4. **Selectors**: Selectors are pure functions used to obtain slices of state from the store. They allow for better separation of concerns and reduce code duplication.

```typescript
import { createFeatureSelector,
createSelector } from '@ngrx/store';

const selectItemsState =
createFeatureSelector<ItemState>('items');

export const selectAllItems =
createSelector(
  selectItemsState,
  (state: ItemState) => state.items
```

```
);
```
```

5. **Effects**: NgRx Effects provide a way
to handle side effects (like making HTTP
requests) in a reactive manner. Actions that
trigger asynchronous operations can be
handled and related actions can be dispatched
based on the result.

```typescript
import { Injectable } from '@angular/core';
import { Actions, createEffect, ofType }
from '@ngrx/effects';
import { ItemService } from
'../services/item.service';
import { loadItems, loadItemsSuccess }
from './item.actions';
import { map, switchMap } from
'rxjs/operators';

@Injectable()
export class ItemEffects {
  constructor(private actions$: Actions,
private itemService: ItemService) {}

  loadItems$ = createEffect(() =>
```
```

```
    this.actions$.pipe(
      ofType(loadItems),
      switchMap(() =>
        this.itemService.getItems().pipe(
          map(items =>
loadItemsSuccess({ items }))
        )
      )
    );
  }
```

When to Use NgRx

While NgRx can significantly add power and
structure to larger applications, it might be
overkill for smaller applications or those with
simple state management needs. Developers
should consider using NgRx when:

- The application state is complex.
- The application needs to manage a lot of
data interactions and asynchronous processes.
- Side effects (such as data fetching, logging,
etc.) need to be controlled and managed
separately.

- The size of the application makes using services for state management insufficient.

Integration with Angular

To integrate NgRx into an Angular application, it involves the following steps:

1. **Install NgRx**: You can install NgRx using the Angular CLI:

```bash
ng add @ngrx/store
ng add @ngrx/effects
```

2. **Setup Store Module**: Import the `StoreModule` into your application's `AppModule`:

```typescript
import { StoreModule } from '@ngrx/store';
import { reducer as itemReducer } from './state/item.reducer';

@NgModule({
  imports: [StoreModule.forRoot({ items:
```

itemReducer })]
  })
  export class AppModule {}
  ```

3. **Creating the State and Reducer**: Define the state interface, create actions, set up the reducer, and handle actions.

4. **Using Store in Components**: Inject the store into your components and use it to dispatch actions and select state slices.

```typescript
import { Store } from '@ngrx/store';
import { loadItems } from './state/item.actions';

constructor(private store: Store) {}

ngOnInit() {
  this.store.dispatch(loadItems());
}
```

NgRx helps manage state in Angular applications effectively, fostering code
```

maintainability and testability by adhering to the principles of functional programming and reactive programming.

Internationalization (i18n)

What is Internationalization?

Internationalization, commonly abbreviated as i18n, is the process of designing your application so that it can be adapted to various languages and regions without requiring engineering changes. Angular provides a built-in mechanism for i18n which facilitates language translation, making it easier for developers to create applications for a global audience.

Key Concepts of Angular i18n

1. **Translation Files**: Angular uses translation files that contain key-value pairs where the key represents the text identifier and the value represents the translated text. These files typically exist in the format of XLIFF or JSON.

For example, a translation file in JSON might look like:

```json
{
  "HELLO": "Hello",
  "WELCOME": "Welcome to our application!",
  "GOODBYE": "Goodbye!"
}
```

2. **Marking Translatable Text**: In your Angular templates, you can mark strings for translation using the `i18n` attribute.

```html
<h1 i18n="@@helloMessage">Hello, World!</h1>
<p i18n="@@welcomeMessage">Welcome to our application!</p>
```

3. **Using the Angular CLI for i18n**: The Angular CLI provides commands to extract translatable strings from the source code and to build the application with the required

localization settings.

- To extract i18n strings:

```bash
ng xi18n --output-path src/locale
```

- To build the application for a specific locale:

```bash
ng build --localize
```

4. **Locale Data**: Angular also provides built-in locale data that helps in formatting numbers, currencies, and dates based on the selected locale.

```typescript
import { registerLocaleData } from '@angular/common';
import localeFr from '@angular/common/locales/fr';

registerLocaleData(localeFr);
```

```

5. **Language Switching**: To support switching between multiple languages at runtime, developers can implement a language service that loads translation files dynamically based on user selection.

### Best Practices for i18n in Angular

1. **Consistent Key Naming**: Create a consistent naming convention for your translation keys to make them easily identifiable and manageable.

2. **Provide Context**: Use comments in your translation files to provide context to translators about how the texts should be interpreted.

3. **Test Localizations**: Regularly test your application with different locales during development to catch any issues early, such as layout problems caused by long translations.

4. **Update Translations**: As the application grows, keep track of new strings
```

and regularly update your translation files.

5. **User Preferences**: If your application requires user preferences for languages, you can store the selected language using a service or local storage, fetching the corresponding translation files based on the stored preference.

Universal (Server-Side Rendering)

What is Angular Universal?

Angular Universal is a technology that allows developers to run Angular applications on the server instead of in the browser. This approach is known as Server-Side Rendering (SSR), and it provides several benefits, including improved performance, better SEO (Search Engine Optimization), and a faster time to first paint (TTFP) for users.

Benefits of Server-Side Rendering

1. **Improved SEO**: Since search engines can easily parse HTML content, SSR can make the application more discoverable. It

improves the chances of indexing content that would otherwise be dynamically generated and not visible to crawlers.

2. **Faster Initial Load**: SSR sends a fully rendered page to the client, improving the perceived performance as the user can see content more quickly.

3. **Better User Experience**: Users on slower internet connections can start viewing content while the application is still loading, enhancing overall performance.

Implementing Angular Universal

To implement Angular Universal in your Angular application, follow these steps:

1. **Add Angular Universal**:

   Use the Angular CLI to add Angular Universal:

   ```bash
   ng add @nguniversal/express-engine
   ```

This command sets up the necessary files and configurations for server-side rendering.

2. **Server Configuration**:

After installation, a new file — typically named `server.ts` — will be created. This file contains configuration for the Express server that will handle incoming requests and render your Angular application.

```typescript
import 'zone.js/dist/zone-node';
import { enableProdMode } from '@angular/core';
import { ngExpressEngine } from '@nguniversal/express-engine';
import * as express from 'express';
import { join } from 'path';

enableProdMode();

const app = express();

const PORT = process.env.PORT || 4000;
const DIST_FOLDER = join(process.cwd(),
```

```
'dist/browser');

  app.engine('html', ngExpressEngine({
    bootstrap: AppServerModuleNgFactory,
  }));

  app.set('view engine', 'html');
  app.set('views', DIST_FOLDER);

  // Serve static files
  app.get('*.*',
express.static(DIST_FOLDER));

  // All regular routes use the Universal engine
  app.get('*', (req, res) => {
    res.render('index', { req });
  });

  app.listen(PORT, () => {
    console.log(`Node server listening on
http://localhost:${PORT}`);
  });
  ```
```

3. **Build the Application**:

Run the following command to build your
```

application for both server and client:

```bash
npm run build:ssr
```

4. **Run Server-Side Rendered Application**:

After building your application, you can serve it using:

```bash
npm run serve:ssr
```

Best Practices for SSR in Angular

1. **Be Mindful of State**: Ensure that you do not execute client-specific code on the server. Use environment checks to prevent executing browser-specific code (like accessing the `window` or `document` object).

```typescript
if (isPlatformBrowser(this.platformId)) {
  // Client-specific code here
```

```
    }
    ```
```

2. **Avoid Blocking Operations**: Heavy computations or long-running processes on the server can slow down the response. Offload heavy computation tasks to background jobs or leverage caching mechanisms.

3. **Use Caching**: Implement caching strategies to store rendered pages and optimize performance for returning users and frequently accessed routes.

4. **Optimize Assets**: Optimize CSS, JavaScript, and images to reduce the initial load time.

5. **Test Performance**: Monitor your server response times and user interactions to understand performance bottlenecks and optimize them accordingly.

Angular is not only limited to building client-
```

side applications; it also supports advanced techniques that can enhance the user experience and performance of web applications. By utilizing state management with NgRx, internationalization for expanding the audience reach, and Server-Side Rendering for improved performance and SEO, developers can create highly efficient, maintainable, and user-friendly Angular applications. Each of these advanced topics brings capabilities that make Angular a comprehensive choice for modern web application development. Embracing these techniques will ensure that your applications stay relevant in an ever-evolving web landscape.

14. Angular syntax

1. **Templates**
Templates in Angular are HTML files that can include Angular-specific syntax. This syntax allows you to embed expressions, directives, and more:

- **Interpolation**: This is used for one-way data binding by embedding expressions into strings. For example:
    ```html
    <h1>{{ title }}</h1>
    ```

In this case, `{{ title }}` is an expression that binds to a property of the component.

- **Directives**: Angular has built-in structural and attribute directives which modify the layout or behavior of elements in templates.
    - **Structural Directives**: These change the structure of the DOM. Common ones include:
        - `*ngIf`: Conditional rendering.
        ```html
```

```html
<div *ngIf="isVisible">Content visible</div>
```

  - `*ngFor`: Looping through a collection.
```html
<ul>
  <li *ngFor="let item of items">{{ item }}</li>
</ul>
```

- **Attribute Directives**: These change the appearance or behavior of an element.
```html
<div [style.backgroundColor]="color">Styled Div</div>
```

2. **Components**
Components are the building blocks of Angular applications. Each component encapsulates its own view (template), data (class), and styles.

- **Component Decorator**: The `@Component` decorator is used to define a component with its metadata.

```typescript
import { Component } from '@angular/core';

@Component({
  selector: 'app-my-component',
  templateUrl: './my-component.component.html',
  styleUrls: ['./my-component.component.css']
})
export class MyComponent {
  title = 'Hello, Angular!';
}
```

3. **Data Binding**
Angular provides several ways to bind data between the component and the template:

- **One-Way Data Binding**:
  1. **Interpolation**: As described above, for displaying component data in templates.

  2. **Property Binding**: Binding a property of a DOM element to a field in the

component.
```html
<img [src]="imageUrl">
```

- **Two-Way Data Binding**: This is achieved using `[(ngModel)]`, allowing for both display of data and the ability to update it.
```html
<input [(ngModel)]="username">
```

To use `ngModel`, you need to import the `FormsModule` in your Angular module.

4. **Pipes**
Pipes are a way to transform data for display in templates. Angular includes built-in pipes like `DatePipe`, `CurrencyPipe`, etc. You can also create custom pipes.
```html
<p>{{ birthday | date:'longDate' }}</p>
```

5. **Services and Dependency Injection**

Services are used to encapsulate business logic, making it reusable across different components. Angular's dependency injection allows you to easily provide services to components.

- **Creating a service**:
  ```typescript
  import { Injectable } from '@angular/core';

  @Injectable({
    providedIn: 'root'
  })
  export class DataService {
    getData() {
      return ['Data1', 'Data2', 'Data3'];
    }
  }
  ```

- **Injecting a service into a component**:
  ```typescript
  import { DataService } from './data.service';

  export class MyComponent {
    constructor(private dataService: DataService) {}
  ```

```
}
```
```
```

Understanding the syntax in Angular is essential for building robust web applications. The syntax for templates, components, data binding, and services provides the means to create dynamic and maintainable applications effectively. Mastering these concepts allows developers to leverage Angular's full potential in their projects.

Angular Glossary

1. **Angular**: A platform and framework for building client-side applications using HTML, CSS, and JavaScript/TypeScript. It enables developers to create single-page applications (SPAs) with a modular architecture.

2. **Component**: The fundamental building block of Angular applications. A component

controls a patch of screen called a view and has associated templates for its HTML layout and styling. Each component encapsulates data, templates, and behavior.

3. **Module**: A container that groups related components, directives, pipes, and services. Every Angular application has at least one module, the root module, typically named `AppModule`.

4. **Service**: A class that encapsulates business logic, data management, or any reusable functionality that can be shared across components. Services are typically used to fetch data from APIs or manage state.

5. **Dependency Injection (DI)**: A design pattern used in Angular to provide components and services with the necessary dependencies without hardcoding them. DI improves modularity and testability.

6. **Directive**: A class that modifies the behavior or appearance of elements in the DOM. Angular provides three types of directives: components, structural directives

(like `*ngIf` and `*ngFor`), and attribute directives.

7. **Pipe**: An Angular class that transforms data for display in templates. Pipes take in data and return a transformed value. Examples include `DatePipe`, `CurrencyPipe`, and custom pipes.

8. **Template**: The HTML view associated with a component. Templates can contain Angular-specific syntax, including directives and binding expressions.

9. **Binding**: A way to connect component data and the template. Angular supports various types of binding, including:
   - **Interpolation**: Binds component properties to the template using double curly braces ({{ }})
   - **Property Binding**: Binds a property of an element to a component property [property]="expression"
   - **Event Binding**: Handles events triggered by user interactions (e.g., (click)="method()")
   - **Two-way Binding**: Combines

property binding and event binding with
`[(ngModel)]` syntax.

10. **Routing**: The mechanism that enables navigation between different views or components in an Angular application. It allows developers to define various routes and their corresponding components.

11. **Observable**: A key part of Angular's reactive programming model. Observables are objects that emit values over time and allow for asynchronous data handling. They are commonly used with Angular's HttpClient module.

12. **RxJS**: A library for reactive programming using Observables. Angular leverages RxJS for event handling, asynchronous programming, and managing data streams.

13. **Form Control**: Represents a single input field in a form. Form controls can be managed in reactive or template-driven forms.

14. **Reactive Forms**: A way to build

forms in Angular using reactive patterns. Reactive forms use the `FormGroup` and `FormControl` classes to create form models.

15. **Template-driven Forms**: An Angular approach to building forms in which forms are defined declaratively in the template using directives like `ngModel`.

16. **Change Detection**: The mechanism by which Angular checks for changes in the component state and updates the UI accordingly. Angular uses a tree of components to efficiently detect changes using strategies like Default and OnPush.

17. **NgModule**: A decorator that marks a class as an Angular module, defining the components, directives, pipes, and services that belong to the module.

18. **CLI (Command Line Interface)**: A command-line tool provided by Angular to create, develop, and maintain Angular applications efficiently. The CLI provides commands for generating components, services, and other aspects of an Angular app.

19. **AOT (Ahead-of-Time Compilation)**: A feature that compiles Angular applications at build time, resulting in faster rendering and better performance in production.

20. **JIT (Just-in-Time Compilation)**: A compilation process that compiles the application in the browser at runtime. Typically used during development for quick testing.

21. **NgZone**: A service that allows developers to manage change detection and the execution context of asynchronous operations.

22. **Lazy Loading**: A technique in Angular where modules are loaded on demand rather than at startup. This optimizes application performance by reducing initial load times.

23. **Interceptor**: A service that can be used to modify HTTP requests and responses. Interceptors can be registered to add headers, handle errors, or log requests.
24. **Environment Variables**:

Configuration settings specific to different environments (development, production, etc.) that can influence application behavior.

25. **State Management**: The practice of managing the state of an application. Angular applications can use services or libraries like NgRx or Akita to maintain application state.

This glossary provides a foundational understanding of key Angular concepts and terminology. Whether you are just starting with Angular or are an experienced developer, familiarity with these terms will help you navigate the Angular ecosystem effectively.

Index

1.Introduction to Dart pg.4

2.Setting up Angular pg.6

3.Angular Components pg.9

4.Angular Directives are markers on a DOM pg.15

5.Angular services pg.20

6.Routing in Angular pg.25

7.Forms in Angular pg.30

8.HTTP Client in Angular pg.36

9.Angular Modules pg. 41

10.Angular Best Practices pg.53

11.Testing in Angular pg.64

12.Deployment of Angular Applications pg.76

13.Advanced Topics in Angular pg.89

14.Angular syntax pg.108